I0837472

Ferenc Margitics - Erika Figula - Zsuzsa Pauwlik

Cyberbully and Cybervictimization in Schools

Cyberbully and Cybervictimization in Schools

Authors:
Dr. Ferenc Margitics Ph.D.,
Dr. Erika Figula Ph.D.,
Dr. Zsuzsa Pauwlik Ph.D.
(margitics.ferenc@nye.hu)

Published by:
Ervin Kery (editor@kery.org)

ISBN: 9798632157148

Contents

Preface 7
Introduction.. 9
       What is cyberbullying? 9
       Types of cyberbullying 12
       Incidence of cyberbullying 15
       Traditional bullying and
       cyberbullying 17
       Cyber Bully Scale 20
       Cyber Victim Scale 21
Methods 22
       Sample 22
       Research tools 23
The Prevalence of Cyber-victimization 47
Summary... 68
References... 74
Appendix... 81
       Cyber Bully Scale 81
       Cyber Victim Scale 84

Preface

During the past decades, the rapid advances in information and communication technology, the development of Wi-Fi network coverage have enabled anyone using a laptop, a tablet or a smartphone to connect quickly to the Internet.

The world wide web has become the cornerstone of social connection, with emails, social networking sites and chat rooms becoming the scenes of social interaction, which have thus become increasingly important in the daily lives of children and adolescents.

As a result of this, new forms of school violence have emerged in primary and secondary schools alongside the traditional ones.

Students are increasingly using information and communication technologies as a means of harassing other people. In this case, we are talking about Internet harassment (cyberbullying).

These violent behaviours can be accomplished by the students through mobile phones, emails, Internet chats and online spaces such as MySpace, Facebook, Instagram, Twitter and personal blogs.

However, cyberbullying, which is often ignored or treated as harmless by pedagogues, can in many cases have more serious consequences for adolescent personality development than the different forms of traditional school violence could.

Online anonymity and the security of hiding behind a computer screen frees the adolescent from traditional barriers and social pressures, as well as moral and ethical concerns.

Thus, adolescents who do not behave violently at school can become cyberbullies in the Internet environment. Anonymity also means the absence of consequences, since cyberbullies are often not identifiable and punishment can, therefore, be avoided.

Our research team has conducted cyberbullying research since 2018. Our goal is to develop a cyberbullying measurement tool and to explore the prevalence and background factors of the phenomenon.

The initial results of our research are summarized in this book.

Introduction

What is cyberbullying?

Internet harassment (cyberbullying) among school students refers to the use of information and communication technologies by primary or secondary school students as a means of harassing their fellow students.

In the words of Belsey (2007), cyberbullying is the malicious and repeated use of information and communication technologies by an individual or a group to threaten other people.

Cyberbullying is manifested in a variety of ways by contacting other people through the Internet or mobile phones.

According to Shariff and Gouin (2005), cyberbullying is a form of psychological intimidation with electronic devices such as mobile phones, blogs, websites, and chat rooms.

Lacey (2007) found out that the most common forms of cyberbullying among students are sending offensive messages, pranking, spreading rumours, humiliation and physical threats.

According to research by Ponsford (2007), the most common forms of cyberbullying among girls are sharing secrets, spreading rumours about others in a virtual environment, attacking their personality or sexual identity, and displaying their classmates as untrustworthy.

While some researchers believe that cyberbullying is an extension of traditional bullying in schools, it has many differences compared with the traditional forms of bullying between schoolmates.

During traditional harassment, the harasser and the victim usually know each other. In the case of cyberbullying, the bully knows who the victim is, but the victim has no idea who is conducting the bullying. Cyberbullying is therefore largely anonymous (Belsey, 2007; Shariff and Gouin, 2005; Slonje and Smith, 2008).

In the cyberspace, the Internet bully can remain anonymous to both the victim and the outside observers (Kowalski, et al, 2008).

Online anonymity and the security of hiding behind a computer screen frees the individual from traditional barriers and social pressures, as well as moral and ethical concerns (Hinduja and Patchin, 2008; Li, 2007).

In this way, adolescents who do not behave violently face to face may become Internet bullies in an online environment. Anonymity also means the absence of consequences, as bullies are often not identifiable and can thus avoid punishment.

While traditional harassment is often limited to a small group, during cyberbullying, the bully can quickly and widely disseminate negative information about the victim to the general public (Slonje and Smith, 2008).

Bullying on the Internet can extend to a degree which is not typical of traditional bullying. For example, an offensive message or image in the form of an Internet virus or embedded in an Internet meme can reach thousands of users. This creates a snowball effect in which harassment is continuously reproduced and disseminated by the secondary uploaders (Slonje et al., 2013).

Hanewald (2008) pointed out that cyberbullying occurs not only at school but also outside school hours.

Therefore, cyberbullying is not limited to the school day, but may occur at any time during the day or night, which increases the vulnerability of children. Thus, cyberbullying goes far beyond schools and may mean that there is no safe haven for children even at home. (Kowalski and Limber, 2007).

Types of cyberbullying

As cyberbullying is a relatively new phenomenon, no consensus has yet been reached on how to categorize it.

Studies published so far include different classifications of cyberbullying.

Smith et al. (2008) classify cyberbullying by media type, that is, they distinguish between cyberbullying via SMS, e-mail, and messenger.

Ortega et al. (2007) propose a classification by type of action.

Willard (2006) divides some forms of cyberbullying into the following categories:

> - sending messages to the victim in an hostile and vulgar language;

> - sending offensive images or rumours of others to tarnish the victim's reputation or social relationships;

> hacking someone's online account to send messages which harm the victim and damage his or her reputation and personal relationships;

> disseminating secrets or disturbing information about the victim;

> deliberate exclusion of the victim from an online group;

> sending intimidating messages to the victim repeatedly.

However, not all of the above behaviours can be considered cyberbullying, bearing in mind that harassment always requires the repetition criterion.

Willard (2006) herself acknowledges this fact by pointing out that some of the forms of harassment she lists may be called "online social cruelty".

According to Riebel et al. (2009), the strict definition of cyberbullying applies only to four of the subtypes identified by Willard. These are the following:

> sending offensive or threatening messages to the victim repeatedly via email, SMS, instant messaging, or chat rooms;

> ➢ spreading rumours about the victim through electronic means of communication. (Unlike real-world rumours, information can be sent to thousands of people over the Internet in seconds);

> ➢ a message revealing personal information sent by the victim to someone in confidence is passed on to other people to endanger the victim;

> ➢ expelling or excluding the victim from multiplayer games, chats or online interfaces.

Langos and Sarre (2015) consider a few other categories worth mentioning:

> ➢ cyberstalking (an extreme harassment, threatening the victim to an extent which endangers his or her safety and leads to a constant sense of fear);

> ➢ happy slapping (capturing a victim's offence in a photo or video, which in many cases may be sexually explicit, and later publicly distributing it to inflict harassing defamation);

> ➢ outing (in which the bully

manipulates the victim with certain personal information, which he or she then discloses to humiliate the victim);

➢ impersonation (the bully pretends to be the victim and sends offensive messages to certain individuals or institutions on his or her behalf as if they were from the victim).

Incidence of cyberbullying

A series of studies warn of the high incidence rate of cyberbullying among adolescents.

According to the research by Ybarra and Mitchell (2004), 12% of adolescents have already been involved as bullies in cyberbullying.

The research by Arıcak (2009) found out that 19.7% of students had been a perpetrator of cyberbullying at least once, while 54.4% had been a victim of cyberbullying at least once.

Li (2006) found out that among secondary school students, 22% of boys and 12% of girls had admitted to harassing others by using computer devices.

According to Ybarra et al. (2007), 64% of the surveyed young people were victims of cyberbullying.

According to the results of research by Raskauskas and Stoltz (2007), 49% of students in the 13-18 age group, while, according to the research by Patchin and Hinduja (2006) in the same age group, 29% of students have been victims of cyberbullying.

In a study conducted by Arıcak et al. (2008) among Turkish students, 35.7% of students admitted the existence of cyberbullying.

Ortega et al. (2008) found out that in Spain, 5.7% of adolescents admitted that they occasionally, whereas 1.7% of them more frequently, committed cyberbullying.

Adams (2010), while investigating victimization according to genders on the Internet, found out that more adolescent girls (25.8%) had reported cyberbullying than boys (16%).

The research by Keith and Martin (2005) also shows that women are more likely to engage in cyberbullying than men.

Humphrey and Symes (2010) found out that students who deal with cognitive, communicative, emotional, and physical challenges are more exposed to traditional and cyberbullying, both within and outside of school.

Traditional bullying and cyberbullying

Numerous studies have shown that cyberbullying leads to aggression. (Arıcak, 2009; Dilmaç, 2009; Harman et al., 2005; Ybarra et al., 2007).

One form of traditional harassment is indirect intimidation, which denotes relational or social aggression when the victim is harmed by other people manipulating their relationships (Björkqvist, 2001).

In this type of aggression, harassers use covert strategies to exclude their competitors and isolate them in their age-group. These activities include spreading disparaging news, threatening interpersonal relationships, and disclosing private information and secrets (Crick, 1995; Galen and Underwood, 1997).

In this sense, certain forms of cyberbullying have the same characteristics as traditional indirect intimidation (Dehue, et al., 2008).

Another important aspect to be mentioned in this topic is the asymmetry of power. In the case of traditional school violence, there must be an imbalance between the harasser and the victim, to the benefit of the harasser, in terms of physical strength and socio-economic status respectively, without which the harassment cannot happen. (Olweus, 1978).

In the case of cyberbullying, such conditions are no longer required. The victim of cyberbullying can often be in an equal or higher position of power than the bully. Students who generally do not actively participate in traditional school violence may be Internet bullies themselves in cyberspace (Vandebosch and Cleemput, 2008).

Vandebosch and Cleemput (2008) found out in a research conducted in the 10-18 age-group that among the motives for committing cyberbullying, revenge, boredom, and curiosity were the most prominent ones.

Cyber Bully and Victim Scale

Questionnaires and scales are the most important tools to measure cyberbullying.

Arıcak et al. (2008) developed a special scale to measure cyberbullying. This scale consists of 21 items designed to measure cyberbullying and how it is expressed.

Another scale applied to measure cyberbullying was developed by Li (2005). The scale consists of 15 items and measures exposure to cyberbullying.

The Cyber Bullying Inventory (CBI) was developed by Erdur-Baker and first used by Erdur-Baker and Kavsut (2007). The CBI consisted of two scales; one measures cyberbullying and the other measures becoming a victim of cyberbullying. There were 16 items on the cyberbullying scale and 18 on the cyber victimization scale.

Students were asked to rate themselves on a 4-point Likert-type scale (1 = It has never happened to me, 2 = It has happened once or twice, 3 = It has happened three-five times, 4 = It has happened more than five times).

In this chapter, we present the Cyber Bully Scale and the Cyber Victim Scale as developed by our research team.

Cyber Bully Scale

The CBS describes 14 forms of cyberbullying, such as bullying on a mobile phone, sharing a victim's secrets on the net, sending abusive, threatening or intimidating messages to a victim, or sharing them on social online platforms, etc.

The occurrence of each form of cyberbullying should be assessed on a Likert-type scale which has the following values:

never (0),

sometimes (1),

often (2),

almost always (3).

We ascertained that Cronbach's alpha, expressing the intrinsic reliability of the CBS scale, was high (0.89) in a representative sample of 882 people.

The complete CBS can be found in the appendix.

Cyber Victim Scale

The Internet Victim Scale (CVS) was developed taking into account the forms of cyberbullying described by Willard (2006), Riebel et al. (2009) and Langos and Sarre (2015).

CVS describes 14 forms of exposure to cyberbullying, such as anonymous mobile phone calls, the distribution of personal information online that the victim would not have wanted others to know, receiving abusive, harassing anonymous emails, or sharing them by others on social platforms, etc.

Exposure to each form of cyberbullying should be assessed by the students on a Likert-type scale which has the following values:

never (0), sometimes (1), often (2), almost always (3).

We ascertained that Cronbach's alpha, expressing the intrinsic reliability of the CBS scale, was high (0.87) in a representative sample of 882 people.

The complete CVS can be found in the appendix.

Methods

In our research, we endeavoured to determine the prevalence of cyberbullying in upper primary and secondary schools.

Sample

The data collection took place in four municipal primary and secondary schools in Nyíregyháza, in two small-town primary and secondary schools in each of the following towns, Vásárosnamény, Mátészalka, and Kisvárda, as well as in eight micro-regional and village primary and secondary schools.

882 students (432 boys and 450 girls) were involved in the research.

The breakdown by school type was as follows:

- ➢ 461 upper primary school students (224 boys and 237 girls);
- ➢ 421 secondary school students (208 boys and 213 girls).

The average age was

- ➢ 12.8 years in primary schools;
- ➢ 16.4 years in secondary schools.

Research tools

We used the Cyber Bully Scale (CBS) and the Cyber Victim Scale (CVS) developed by our research team to measure the prevalence of cyberbullying.

The Prevalence of Cyberbully

According to the results of our research, 63.4% of primary school students have already participated in some form of cyberbullying.

Table 1 shows the percentage of responses to each item on the Cyber Bully Scale (CBS) based on a sample of primary school students.

		1	2	3	S*
1	I sent emails to some of my classmates in which I mocked or made them uncomfortable.	5,1	0,8	0,9	6,8
2	I uploaded videos about some of my classmates to You Tube that were funny for the others.	2,9	0,8	0,6	4,3
3	When I became aware of them, I was happy to share the secrets of others on the net.	4,1	1,5	1,7	7,3
4	I sent an annoying anonymous message to one of my classmates (text, picture, video) via email, SMS, chat or social network site.	4,8	0,9	0,9	6,6
5	I logged into the personal user account of one of my classmates (email, social network, etc.)	7,7	1,5	0,9	10,1

6	I impersonated the online personality of one of my classmates (email, community site, etc.).	4,2	1,2	0,8	6,2
7	I edited a picture or video of one of my classmates that puts him or her in a ridiculous, humiliating position, and distributed it online.	5,9	0,8	0,6	7,3
8	I have already called my classmate anonymously on a mobile phone.	15,9	4,2	2,4	22,5
9	I created a website or blog about one of my classmates in order to discredit him or her to others.	0,8	0,6	0,2	1,6
10	I hacked and modified a personal website or blog of one of my classmates.	3	0,3	0,8	4,1
11	I falsely informed an ISP to exclude one of my classmates from the online service.	1,5	0,8	0,2	2,5
12	I spread malicious rumors about my classmates using online tools.	3,9	1,1	0,3	5,3
13	I blocked one of my classmate's online access- for example, by changing the password.	4,5	1,2	0,3	6

14	I ignored some of my classmates in an online environment.	21,9	5,9	5,4	33,2

* 1. Sometimes, 2. Often, 3. Almost always, S. Summary

Table 1. *The percentage of responses to the items on the Cyber Bully Scale (CBS) among primary school students.*

The most common form of cyberbullying among primary school students was social exclusion in an online environment in 33,2% of the cases. (I ignored some of my classmates in an online environment.).

This was followed by harassment using a mobile phone (22.5%) and hacking of an online account to send emails that could cause problems for the victim (10.1%).

We found out that the least characteristic of this age group were creating a website or blog in the name of another person to discredit that person (1.6%), falsely informing an ISP for exclusion (2.5%), and hacking and modifying a personal blog (4.1%).

Examining primary school students by gender, we found out that 59.9% of girls and 67% of boys had already been cyberbullies.

Table 2 shows the total percentage of responses to the Cyber Bully Scale (CBS) items by gender in the primary school student sample.

		Boys	Girls
1	I sent emails to some of my classmates in which I mocked or made them uncomfortable.	9,6	4
2	I uploaded videos about some of my classmates to You Tube that were funny for the others.	6,6	1,5
3	When I became aware of them, I was happy to share the secrets of others on the net.	10,2	4,3
4	I sent an annoying anonymous message to one of my classmates (text, picture, video) via email, SMS, chat or social network site.	10,2	3,1
5	I logged into the personal user account of one of my classmates (email, social network, etc.)	12,3	7,7
6	I impersonated the online personality of one of my classmates (email, community site, etc.).	8,1	4,3
7	I edited a picture or video of one of my classmates that puts him or her in a ridiculous, humiliating position, and distributed it online.	11,2	3,1
8	I have already called my classmate anonymously on a mobile phone.	26,2	18,8

9	I created a website or blog about one of my classmates in order to discredit him or her to others.	2,4	0,6
10	I hacked and modified a personal website or blog of one of my classmates.	5,7	2,5
11	I falsely informed an ISP to exclude one of my classmates from the online service.	4,2	0,6
12	I spread malicious rumors about my classmates using online tools.	8,1	2,5
13	I blocked one of my classmate's online access- for example, by changing the password.	9,6	2,1
14	I ignored some of my classmates in an online environment.	34	35

Table 2. *Total percentage of responses to items on the Cyber Bully Scale (CBS) by gender among primary school students.*

Among girls in primary schools, the most common forms of cyberbullying were social exclusion in the 35% of the cases in an online environment (I ignored some of my classmates in an online environment.) and harassment using a mobile phone (18.8%).

In this age group, we found out that girls are the least likely to falsely inform an ISP for exclusion (0.6%), to create a website or blog in the name of another person to discredit that person (0.6%) and to hack and modify a personal blog (2.1%).

Among boys in primary schools, the most common form of cyberbullying was also social exclusion in 34% of the cases in an online environment (I ignored some of my classmates in an online environment).

This was followed by harassment using a mobile phone (26.5%), hacking someone's online account, hacking to send email messages that may cause problems for the victim (12.3%), editing and distributing offensive images of others (11.2%), as well as sending bothersome messages (10.2%) or spreading rumours about others (10.2%).

In this age group, the least characteristic for boys was to create a website or a blog in the name of another person to discredit that person (2.4%) and to falsely inform an ISP for exclusion (4.2%).

The results of the gender comparative statistical test (two-sample t-test) for the primary school sample are presented in Table 3 (the table only shows those types of harassment where we found a significant difference between the two samples).

		t.	sig.
1	I sent emails to some of my classmates in which I mocked or made them uncomfortable.	2,469	0,014
2	I uploaded videos about some of my classmates to You Tube that were funny for the others.	3,584	0,000
3	When I became aware of them, I was happy to share the secrets of others on the net.	3,092	0,002
4	I sent an annoying anonymous message to one of my classmates (text, picture, video) via email, SMS, chat or social network site.	3,452	0,001
5	I logged into the personal user account of one of my classmates (email, social network, etc.)	2,654	0,008
6	I impersonated the online personality of one of my classmates (email, community site, etc.).	2,606	0,009
7	I edited a picture or video of one of my classmates that puts him or her in a ridiculous, humiliating position, and distributed it online.	3,939	0,000
8	I have already called my classmate anonymously on a mobile phone.	2,962	0,003
10	I created a website or blog about one of my classmates in order to discredit him or her to others.	2,187	0,029

11	I hacked and modified a personal website or blog of one of my classmates.	2,366	0,018
12	I falsely informed an ISP to exclude one of my classmates from the online service.	3,553	0,000
13	I spread malicious rumors about my classmates using online tools.	4,068	0,000

Table 3. *Results of the gender comparative statistical study (two-sample t-test) (primary school sample).*

According to the results of the gender comparative statistical study, the following forms of cyberbullying were found to be significantly more characteristic for boys in primary schools:

> sending hostile and harassing electronic messages;

> editing and sharing offensive pictures, videos;

> dissemination of secrets or confidential information;

> hacking an online account, blog, disabling access to them;

> anonymous phone calls;

> assuming a false online identity;

> ➢ spreading malicious rumours;

> ➢ falsely informing an ISP.

According to our research, 47.5% of secondary school students responded positively to at least one form of harassment.

According to our research, 68.7% of secondary school students have already participated in some form of cyberbullying.

		1	2	3	S*
1	I sent emails to some of my classmates in which I mocked or made them uncomfortable.	9,2	0	0,4	9,6
2	I uploaded videos about some of my classmates to You Tube that were funny for the others.	3,3	0,4	0	3,7
3	When I became aware of them, I was happy to share the secrets of others on the net.	3,3	1,3	0	4,6
4	I sent an annoying anonymous message to one of my classmates (text, picture, video) via email, SMS, chat or social network site.	3,8	0	0,8	4,6
5	I logged into the personal user account of one of my classmates (email, social network, etc.)	4,6	0,4	0,8	5,8

6	I impersonated the online personality of one of my classmates (email, community site, etc.).	4,2	0	0,4	4,6
7	I edited a picture or video of one of my classmates that puts him or her in a ridiculous, humiliating position, and distributed it online.	7,5	0	2,9	10,4
8	I have already called my classmate anonymously on a mobile phone.	18,9	2,9	3,4	25,2
9	I created a website or blog about one of my classmates in order to discredit him or her to others.	0,4	0,4	0	0,8
10	I hacked and modified a personal website or blog of one of my classmates.	3,8	0	0	3,8
11	I falsely informed an ISP to exclude one of my classmates from the online service.	1,3	0	0	1,3
12	I spread malicious rumors about my classmates using online tools.	1,3	0	0,4	1,7
13	I blocked one of my classmate's online access- for example, by changing the password.	4,6	0,8	0	5,4

14	I ignored some of my classmates in an online environment.	24,3	6,7	9,6	40,6

* 1. Sometimes, 2. Often, 3. Almost always, S. Summary

Table 4. *The percentage of responses to the items on the Cyber Bully Scale (CBS) among secondary school students.*

Table 4 shows the percentage of responses to items on the Cyber Bully Scale (CBS) in the sample of secondary school students.

The most common form of cyberbullying among secondary school students was social exclusion in an online environment in 40.6% of the cases. (I ignored some of my classmates in an online environment) .

This was followed by harassment using a mobile phone (25.2%) and editing and sharing offensive images (10.4%).

In this age group, the least characteristic was creating a website or a blog in the name of another person to discredit that person (0.8%), falsely informing an ISP for exclusion (1.3%) and distributing malicious rumours (1.7%).

Examining secondary school students by gender, we found out that 64.5% of girls and 72.8% of boys had already been cyberbullies.

Table 5 shows the total percentage of responses to the Cyber Bully Scale (CBS) items by gender in the secondary school student sample.

		Boys	**Girls**
1	I sent emails to some of my classmates in which I mocked or made them uncomfortable.	11,9	5
2	I uploaded videos about some of my classmates to You Tube that were funny for the others.	5,6	1,2
3	When I became aware of them, I was happy to share the secrets of others on the net.	6,9	1,2
4	I sent an annoying anonymous message to one of my classmates (text, picture, video) via email, SMS, chat or social network site.	5,8	2,5
5	I logged into the personal user account of one of my classmates (email, social network, etc.)	7,6	2,5
6	I impersonated the online personality of one of my classmates (email, community site, etc.).	6,3	1,3
7	I edited a picture or video of one of my classmates that puts him or her in a ridiculous, humiliating position, and distributed it online.	15,3	1,3

8	I have already called my classmate anonymously on a mobile phone.	27,2	21,4
9	I created a website or blog about one of my classmates in order to discredit him or her to others.	1,2	1,2
10	I hacked and modified a personal website or blog of one of my classmates.	5,7	2,5
11	I falsely informed an ISP to exclude one of my classmates from the online service.	1,9	1,2
12	I spread malicious rumors about my classmates using online tools.	2,5	1,2
13	I blocked one of my classmate's online access- for example, by changing the password.	7,6	1,2
14	I ignored some of my classmates in an online environment.	42,7	36,3

Table 5. *Total percentage of responses to items on the Cyber Bully Scale (CBS) by gender among secondary school students.*

Among girls in secondary schools, the most common forms of cyberbullying were social exclusion in the 36.3% of the cases in an online environment (I ignored some of my classmates in an online environment) and harassment using a mobile phone (21.4%).

In this age group, girls were not prone to other forms of cyberbullying, which had prevalence rates of between 1.2% and 5%.

Among high school boys, the most common form of cyberbullying was social exclusion in the 42.7% of the cases in the online environment (I ignored some of my classmates in an online environment).

This was followed by harassment using a mobile phone (27.2%), editing and distributing offensive images of others (15.3%), and sending offensive emails (11.9%).

We found out that the least characteristic forms of cyberbullying for boys of this age group were creating a website or blog in the name of another person to discredit that person (1.2%), falsely informing the ISP (1.9%), and distributing malicious rumours (2.5%).

The results of the gender comparative statistical test (two-sample t-test) for the secondary school sample are presented in Table 6 (the table only shows those types of harassment where we found a significant difference between the two samples).

		t	sig.
1	I sent emails to some of my classmates in which I mocked or made them uncomfortable.	2,342	0,014
2	I uploaded videos about some of my classmates to You Tube that were funny for the others.	2,095	0,037
3	When I became aware of them, I was happy to share the secrets of others on the net.	2,283	0,023
7	I edited a picture or video of one of my classmates that puts him or her in a ridiculous, humiliating position, and distributed it online.	3,000	0,003
10	I hacked and modified a personal website or blog of one of my classmates.	2,175	0,031
13	I blocked one of my classmate's online access- for example, by changing the password.	2,014	0,045

Table 6. *Results of the gender comparative statistical study (two-sample t-test) (secondary school sample).*

The results of a gender-based comparative statistics study show that secondary school boys are significantly more prone to the following forms of cyberbullying:

> ➢ sending hostile and disturbing electronic messages;

> ➢ editing and sharing offensive pictures, videos;

> ➢ dissemination of secrets or confidential information;

> ➢ hacking an online account, blog, disabling access to them.

Table 7 shows the total percentage of responses to items on the Cyber Bully Scale (CBS) by school type in the entire sample.

		Primary	Secondary
1	I sent emails to some of my classmates in which I mocked or made them uncomfortable.	6,8	9,6
2	I uploaded videos about some of my classmates to You Tube that were funny for the others.	4,3	3,7
3	When I became aware of them, I was happy to share the secrets of others on the net.	7,3	4,6
4	I sent an annoying anonymous message to one of my classmates (text, picture, video) via email, SMS, chat or social network site.	6,6	4,6
5	I logged into the personal user account of one of my classmates (email, social network, etc.)	10,1	5,8

6	I impersonated the online personality of one of my classmates (email, community site, etc.).	6,2	4,6
7	I edited a picture or video of one of my classmates that puts him or her in a ridiculous, humiliating position, and distributed it online.	7,3	10,4
8	I have already called my classmate anonymously on a mobile phone.	22,5	25,2
9	I created a website or blog about one of my classmates in order to discredit him or her to others.	1,6	0,8
10	I hacked and modified a personal website or blog of one of my classmates.	4,1	3,8
11	I falsely informed an ISP to exclude one of my classmates from the online service.	2,5	1,3
12	I spread malicious rumors about my classmates using online tools.	5,3	1,7
13	I blocked one of my classmate's online access- for example, by changing the password.	6	5,4
14	I ignored some of my classmates in an online environment.	33,2	40,6

Table 7. *Total percentage of responses to the Cyber Bully Scale (CBS) items by school type*

The results of the comparative statistical test (two-sample t-test) in the whole sample by school type are shown in Table 8 (only the types of harassment in which a significant difference were found between the two samples are shown in the table).

		t.	sig
5	I logged into the personal user account of one of my classmates (email, social network, etc.)	1,981	0,049
12	I spread malicious rumors about my classmates using online tools.	1,970	0,049
14	I ignored some of my classmates in an online environment.	-2,653	0,008

Table 8. *Results of a comparative statistical test (two-sample t-test) between school types (full sample).*

The results show that while, among primary school students, hacking an online account and distributing malicious rumours have prevalence, we found out that among secondary school students, social exclusion is significantly more characteristic.

Table 9 shows the overall percentage of girls who responded to the Cyber Bully Scale (CBS) items by type of school.

		Primary	Secondary
1	I sent emails to some of my classmates in which I mocked or made them uncomfortable.	4	5
2	I uploaded videos about some of my classmates to You Tube that were funny for the others.	1,5	1,2
3	When I became aware of them, I was happy to share the secrets of others on the net.	4,3	1,2
4	I sent an annoying anonymous message to one of my classmates (text, picture, video) via email, SMS, chat or social network site.	3,1	2,5
5	I logged into the personal user account of one of my classmates (email, social network, etc.)	7,7	2,5
6	I impersonated the online personality of one of my classmates (email, community site, etc.).	4,3	1,3
7	I edited a picture or video of one of my classmates that puts him or her in a ridiculous, humiliating position, and distributed it online.	3,1	1,3
8	I have already called my classmate anonymously on a mobile phone.	18,8	21,4

9	I created a website or blog about one of my classmates in order to discredit him or her to others.	0,6	1,2
10	I hacked and modified a personal website or blog of one of my classmates.	2,5	2,5
11	I falsely informed an ISP to exclude one of my classmates from the online service.	0,6	1,2
12	I spread malicious rumors about my classmates using online tools.	2,5	1,2
13	I blocked one of my classmate's online access- for example, by changing the password.	2,1	1,2
14	I ignored some of my classmates in an online environment.	35	36,3

Table 9. *Total percentage of response to Cyber Bully Scale (CBS) items by school type among girls*

According to the results of a comparative statistical test (two-sample t-test) among the sample for girls by school type, we did not find out any significant difference in some forms of cyberbullying between the two age groups.

Table 10 shows the overall percentage of boys who responded to Cyber Bully Scale (CBS) items by school type.

		Primary	Secondary
1	I sent emails to some of my classmates in which I mocked or made them uncomfortable.	9,6	11,9
2	I uploaded videos about some of my classmates to You Tube that were funny for the others.	6,6	5,6
3	When I became aware of them, I was happy to share the secrets of others on the net.	10,2	6,9
4	I sent an annoying anonymous message to one of my classmates (text, picture, video) via email, SMS, chat or social network site.	10,2	5,8
5	I logged into the personal user account of one of my classmates (email, social network, etc.)	12,3	7,6
6	I impersonated the online personality of one of my classmates (email, community site, etc.).	8,1	6,3
7	I edited a picture or video of one of my classmates that puts him or her in a ridiculous, humiliating position, and distributed it online.	11,2	15,3
8	I have already called my classmate anonymously on a mobile phone.	26,2	27,2
9	I created a website or blog about one of my classmates in order to discredit him or her to others.	2,4	1,2

10	I hacked and modified a personal website or blog of one of my classmates.	5,7	5,7
11	I falsely informed an ISP to exclude one of my classmates from the online service.	4,2	1,9
12	I spread malicious rumors about my classmates using online tools.	8,1	2,5
13	I blocked one of my classmate's online access- for example, by changing the password.	9,6	7,6
14	I ignored some of my classmates in an online environment.	34	42,7

Table 10. *Total percentage of response to Cyber Bully Scale (CBS) items by school type among girls*

The results of the comparative statistical test (two-sample t-test) among the sample for boys by school type are shown in Table 11 (this table only shows the types of harassment where we found a significant difference between the two samples).

		t	sig
12	I spread malicious rumors about my classmates using online tools.	2,062	0,040
14	I ignored some of my classmates in an online environment.	-2,029	0,043

Table 11. *Results of a comparative statistical study (two-sample t-test) by school type (boys)*

The results show that while primary school boys were prone to spreading malicious rumours, secondary school students were more significantly prone to online social exclusion.

The Prevalence of Cyber-victimization

According to our research, 68.9% of primary school students have experienced some form of cyberbullying.

Table 12 shows the percentage of responses to items on the Cyber Victim Scale (CVS) in the primary school student sample.

		1	2	3	S*
1	I received emails from some of my classmates that offended me.	10,7	1,8	0,9	13,4
2	My classmates have already uploaded a video of me to YouTube that made me feel uncomfortable.	3	0,6	0,2	3,8
3	Some information about me has been uploaded to the net that I would not have liked if others knew about it.	8,9	2,3	0,6	11,8
4	I received an anonymous message containing harassing content from one of my classmates (text, picture, video) via email, SMS, chat or community site.	6,1	1,8	1,7	9,6
5	One of my classmates has logged in to my personal user account (email, social network, etc.).	6,5	0,8	0,5	6

6	One of my classmates faked my online personality (email, social network, etc.).	4,7	0,8	0,5	6
7	One of my classmates has already edited a picture or video of me that put me in a ridiculous, humiliating position, and disseminated it online.	7,4	0,6	0,2	8,2
8	I have already been called anonymously on a mobile phone, about which I thought my classmates were having fun with me.	21,5	4,8	1,7	28
9	One of my classmates has created a website or blog to discredit me to other people.	1,8	0,3	0,2	2,3
10	My classmates hacked my personal website or blog and modified it.	2,9	0,6	0,3	3,6
11	I have been excluded from an online service because I was falsely reported to the service provider.	2	0,3	0,3	2,6
12	My classmates have been spreading malicious rumours about me using online tools.	7	2	0,6	9,6
13	My classmate blocked my online access - for example, by changing the password.	3	0,3	0,3	3,6

14	Some of my classmates ignored me in an online enviromnment.	16,8	2,3	1,8	23,5

* 1. Sometimes, 2. Often, 3. Almost always, S. Summary

Table 12. *The percentage of responses to the items on the Cyber Victim Scale (CVS) among primary school students.*

Of all forms of cyberbullying, harassment using a mobile phone has been most often experienced at the highest rate (28%).

This was followed by online social exclusion (Some of my classmates ignored me in an online environment.) (23.5%), receiving offensive email messages (13.4%), and unauthorized sharing of personal information (11.8%).

This age-group has least experienced the following forms of harassment:

> Creating a discrediting website or blog (2.3%);

> False complaint exclusion from online service (2.6%);

> Hacking and modifying a personal website or blog (3.6%);

> Blocking online access (3.6%).

Examining primary school students by gender, we found out that 64.7% of girls and 72.6% of boys had been victims of cyberbullying at least once.

Table 13 shows the total percentage of responses to items on the Cyber Victim Scale (CVS) by gender in the primary school student sample.

		Boys	Girls
1	I received emails from some of my classmates that offended me.	13,5	13,5
2	My classmates have already uploaded a video of me to YouTube that made me feel uncomfortable.	6	1,5
3	Some information about me has been uploaded to the net that I would not have liked if others knew about it.	13,8	9,8
4	I received an anonymous message containing harassing content from one of my classmates (text, picture, video) via email, SMS, chat or community site.	10,2	8,8
5	One of my classmates has logged in to my personal user account (email, social network, etc.).	10	5,2
6	One of my classmates faked my online personality (email, social network, etc.).	9	2,8

7	One of my classmates has already edited a picture or video of me that put me in a ridiculous, humiliating position, and disseminated it online.	9,6	6,4
8	I have already been called anonymously on a mobile phone, about which I thought my classmates were having fun with me.	29,3	26,7
9	One of my classmates has created a website or blog to discredit me to other people.	3,3	1,2
10	My classmates hacked my personal website or blog and modified it.	5,4	2,1
11	I have been excluded from an online service because I was falsely reported to the service provider.	4,5	0,6
12	My classmates have been spreading malicious rumours about me using online tools.	10,8	8,3
13	My classmate blocked my online access - for example, by changing the password.	5,1	2,1
14	Some of my classmates ignored me in an online enviromnment.	17,8	23,2

Table 13. *Total percentage of responses to items on the Cyber Victim Scale (CVS) by primary school students by gender.*

Of all forms of cyberbullying, girls in primary schools have most often experienced harassment using a mobile phone, (26.7%), social exclusion in an online environment (I ignored some of my classmates in an online environment)   (18.8%),   and   receiving offensive emails (13.5%).

The following forms of harassment have been least experienced by girls in primary schools:

> False complaint exclusion from online service (0.6%);

> Creating a discrediting website or blog (1.2%);

> Hacking and modifying a personal website or blog (2.1%);

> Blocking online access (2.1%).

Of all forms of cyberbullying, boys (just like girls) in primary schools have most often experienced harassment using a mobile phone (29.3%), and social exclusion in an online environment (23.2%) (I ignored some of my classmates in an online environment).

This was followed by the experience of unauthorized sharing of personal information (13.8%) and receiving offensive emails (13.5%).

The following forms of harassment have been least experienced by boys in primary schools:

➢ Creating a discrediting website or blog (3.3%);

➢ False complaint exclusion from online service (4.5%);

➢ Blocking online access (5.4%);

➢ Hacking and modifying a personal website or blog (5.1%).

The results of the gender comparative statistical test (two-sample t-test) for the primary school sample are presented in Table 14 (the table only shows the exposure patterns for bullying where we found a significant difference between the two samples).

		t.	Sig.
5	One of my classmates has logged in to my personal user account (email, social network, etc.).	2,434	0,015
6	One of my classmates faked my online personality (email, social network, etc.).	3,182	0,002
9	One of my classmates has created a website or blog to discredit me to other people.	2,012	0,045

11	I have been excluded from an online service because I was falsely reported to the service provider.	3,035	0,003
13	My classmate blocked my online access - for example, by changing the password.	2,031	0,043

Table 14. *Results of a comparative statistical study of the sexes (two-sample t-test) (primary school sample)*

The results of a gender-based comparative statistics study show that primary school boys are significantly more likely to experience the following forms of cyberbullying:

➢ hacking an online account, blog, disabling access;

➢ creating a fake website or blog;

➢ assuming a false online identity;

➢ falsely informing an ISP.

According to our research, 72.4% of secondary school students have experienced some form of cyberbullying.

Table 15 shows the percentage of responses to items on the Cyber Victim Scale (CVS) in the secondary school student sample.

		1	2	3	S*
1	I received emails from some of my classmates that offended me.	7,5	1,7	0,8	10
2	My classmates have already uploaded a video of me to YouTube that made me feel uncomfortable.	2,5	0	0	2,5
3	Some information about me has been uploaded to the net that I would not have liked if others knew about it.	6,3	1,7	0,4	8,4
4	I received an anonymous message containing harassing content from one of my classmates (text, picture, video) via email, SMS, chat or community site.	3,4	1,7	0,4	5,5
5	One of my classmates has logged in to my personal user account (email, social network, etc.).	4,6	0,4	0,4	5,4
6	One of my classmates faked my online personality (email, social network, etc.).	2,5	0,4	0,8	3,7
7	One of my classmates has already edited a picture or video of me that put me in a ridiculous, humiliating position, and disseminated it online.	8,4	0,8	0,8	10
8	I have already been called anonymously on a	18,1	7,1	2,1	27,3

		1	2	3	S
	mobile phone, about which I thought my classmates were having fun with me.				
9	One of my classmates has created a website or blog to discredit me to other people.	0,8	0	0	0,8
10	My classmates hacked my personal website or blog and modified it.	2,5	0,4	0	2,9
11	I have been excluded from an online service because I was falsely reported to the service provider.	0,8	1,3	0	2,1
12	My classmates have been spreading malicious rumours about me using online tools.	3,8	1,3	1,3	6,4
13	My classmate blocked my online access - for example, by changing the password.	3	0,4	0,4	3,8
14	Some of my classmates ignored me in an online enviromnment.	14,8	1,7	3,8	20,3

* 1. Sometimes, 2. Often, 3. Almost always, S. Summary

Table 15. *The percentage of responses to the items on the Cyber Victim Scale (CVS) among secondary school students.*

Of all forms of cyberbullying, secondary school students have most commonly experienced harassment using a mobile phone (27.3%).

This was followed by the experiencing exclusion from the online environment (Some of my classmates ignored me) (20.3%), receiving offensive emails (10%), and editing and sharing offensive images (10%).

This age group has least experienced the following forms of harassment :

- ➢ Creating a discrediting website or blog (0.8%);

- ➢ False complaint exclusion from online service (2.1%);

- ➢ Posting an offensive video (2.5%);

- ➢ Hacking and modifying a personal website or blog (2.9%).

Examining high school students by gender, we found out that 67.3% of girls and 76.8% of boys had already been victims of cyberbullying.

Table 16 shows the total percentage of responses to items on the Cyber Victim Scale (CVS) by gender in the secondary school student sample.

		Boys	Girls
1	I received emails from some of my classmates that offended me.	10,1	10,1
2	My classmates have already uploaded a video of me to YouTube that made me feel uncomfortable.	3,8	2,5
3	Some information about me has been uploaded to the net that I would not have liked if others knew about it.	8,8	7,6
4	I received an anonymous message containing harassing content from one of my classmates (text, picture, video) via email, SMS, chat or community site.	4,4	5,1
5	One of my classmates has logged in to my personal user account (email, social network, etc.).	5,6	1,2
6	One of my classmates faked my online personality (email, social network, etc.).	5	1,2
7	One of my classmates has already edited a picture or video of me that put me in a ridiculous, humiliating position, and disseminated it online.	12	6,4

8	I have already been called anonymously on a mobile phone, about which I thought my classmates were having fun with me.	27,7	26,5
9	One of my classmates has created a website or blog to discredit me to other people.	1,3	2,5
10	My classmates hacked my personal website or blog and modified it.	3,1	2,5
11	I have been excluded from an online service because I was falsely reported to the service provider.	3,2	2,5
12	My classmates have been spreading malicious rumours about me using online tools.	5	8,9
13	My classmate blocked my online access - for example, by changing the password.	3,7	3,8
14	Some of my classmates ignored me in an online enviromnment.	23,5	14,9

Table 16. *Total percentage of responses to items on the Cyber Victim Scale (CVS) by secondary school students by gender.*

Of all forms of cyberbullying, secondary school girls have most commonly experienced harassment using a mobile phone (26.5%), online social exclusion (I ignored some of my classmates in an online environment.) (14.9%), and receiving offensive emails (10.1%).

The girls have least commonly become victims of the following forms of cyberbullying:

> Hacking and modifying a personal website or blog (1.2%)

> Blocking online access (1.2%).

Of all forms of cyberbullying, secondary school boys (just like girls) have most commonly experienced harassment using a mobile phone (27.7%), and online social exclusion (I ignored some of my classmates in an online environment) (23.5%).

This was followed by editing and sharing offensive images (12%) and receiving offensive e-mails (10.1%).

The boys have least commonly become victims of the following forms of cyberbullying:

> Creating a discrediting website or blog (1.3%);

> Hacking and modifying a personal website or blog (3.1%);

> False complaint exclusion from online service (3.2%).

According to the results of a comparative statistical test (two-sample t-test) conducted on a sample of secondary school students, no significant difference has been found between the two genders regarding specific forms of cyberbullying.

Table 17 shows the total percentage of responses to items on the Cyber Victim Scale (CVS) per school type in the entire sample.

		Primary	Secondary
1	I received emails from some of my classmates that offended me.	13,4	10
2	My classmates have already uploaded a video of me to YouTube that made me feel uncomfortable.	3,8	2,5
3	Some information about me has been uploaded to the net that I would not have liked if others knew about it.	11,8	8,4
4	I received an anonymous message containing harassing content from one of my classmates (text, picture, video) via email, SMS, chat or community site.	9,6	5,5
5	One of my classmates has logged in to my personal user account (email, social network, etc.).	6	5,4
6	One of my classmates faked my online personality (email, social network, etc.).	6	3,7

7	One of my classmates has already edited a picture or video of me that put me in a ridiculous, humiliating position, and disseminated it online.	8,2	10
8	I have already been called anonymously on a mobile phone, about which I thought my classmates were having fun with me.	28	27,3
9	One of my classmates has created a website or blog to discredit me to other people.	2,3	0,8
10	My classmates hacked my personal website or blog and modified it.	3,6	2,9
11	I have been excluded from an online service because I was falsely reported to the service provider.	2,6	2,1
12	My classmates have been spreading malicious rumours about me using online tools.	9,6	6,4
13	My classmate blocked my online access - for example, by changing the password.	3,6	3,8
14	Some of my classmates ignored me in an online enviromnment.	23,5	20,3

Table 17. Results of a comparative statistical study of the sexes (two-sample t-test) (secondary school sample)

Based on the results of a comparative statistical test (two-sample t-test) of the entire school sample, we have found no significant difference between the two age groups regarding specific forms of cyberbullying.

Table 18 shows the total percentage of responses to items on the Cyber Victim Scale (CVS) per school type among girls.

		Primary	Secondary
1	I received emails from some of my classmates that offended me.	13,5	10,1
2	My classmates have already uploaded a video of me to YouTube that made me feel uncomfortable.	1,5	2,5
3	Some information about me has been uploaded to the net that I would not have liked if others knew about it.	9,8	7,6
4	I received an anonymous message containing harassing content from one of my classmates (text, picture, video) via email, SMS, chat or community site.	8,8	5,1
5	One of my classmates has logged in to my personal user account (email, social network, etc.).	5,2	1,2
6	One of my classmates faked my online personality (email, social network, etc.).	2,8	1,2

7	One of my classmates has already edited a picture or video of me that put me in a ridiculous, humiliating position, and disseminated it online.	6,4	6,4
8	I have already been called anonymously on a mobile phone, about which I thought my classmates were having fun with me.	26,7	26,5
9	One of my classmates has created a website or blog to discredit me to other people.	1,2	2,5
10	My classmates hacked my personal website or blog and modified it.	2,1	2,5
11	I have been excluded from an online service because I was falsely reported to the service provider.	0,6	2,5
12	My classmates have been spreading malicious rumours about me using online tools.	8,3	8,9
13	My classmate blocked my online access - for example, by changing the password.	2,1	3,8
14	Some of my classmates ignored me in an online environmnent.	23,2	14,9

Table 18. *Total percentage of response to Cyber Victim Scale (CVS) items by school type among girls*

The results of a comparative statistical test (two-sample t-test) in the sample of the girls by school type did not show any significant difference between the two age groups regarding specific forms of cyberbullying.

Table 19 shows the total percentages of responses to items on the Cyber Victim Scale (CVS) by school type for boys.

		Primary	Secondary
1	I received emails from some of my classmates that offended me.	13,5	10,1
2	My classmates have already uploaded a video of me to YouTube that made me feel uncomfortable.	6	3,8
3	Some information about me has been uploaded to the net that I would not have liked if others knew about it.	13,8	8,8
4	I received an anonymous message containing harassing content from one of my classmates (text, picture, video) via email, SMS, chat or community site.	10,2	4,4
5	One of my classmates has logged in to my personal user account (email, social network, etc.).	10	5,6
6	One of my classmates faked my online personality (email, social network, etc.).	9	5

7	One of my classmates has already edited a picture or video of me that put me in a ridiculous, humiliating position, and disseminated it online.	9,6	12
8	I have already been called anonymously on a mobile phone, about which I thought my classmates were having fun with me.	29,3	27,7
9	One of my classmates has created a website or blog to discredit me to other people.	3,3	1,3
10	My classmates hacked my personal website or blog and modified it.	5,4	3,1
11	I have been excluded from an online service because I was falsely reported to the service provider.	4,5	3,2
12	My classmates have been spreading malicious rumours about me using online tools.	10,8	5
13	My classmate blocked my online access - for example, by changing the password.	5,1	3,7
14	Some of my classmates ignored me in an online enviromnment.	17,8	23,5

Table 19. *Total percentage of response to Cyber Victim Scale (CVS) items by school type among boys*

The results of a comparative statistical test (two-sample t-test) of boys by school type did not show any significant difference between the two age groups regarding specific forms of Internet bullying.

Summary

In the first part of the book, we have presented the Cyber Bully Scale (CBS) and Victim Scale (CVS) developed by our research team to measure cyberbullying.

The scales which present 14 ways of cyberbullying and 14 ways of falling victim to cyberbullying have excellent psychometric properties in terms of internal consistency.

With the help of the CBS and CVS scales, a representative sample has revealed the incidence of cyberbullying among primary and secondary school students. The results of this are presented in the second part of the book.

We have found that the prevalence of cyberbullying was very high in both types of schools. 63.4% of primary and 68.7% of high school students have been actively involved in cyberbullying.

This rate is much higher than previous research has shown in adolescent samples. (Ybarra and Mitchell, 2004; Li, 2006; Arıcak et al., 2008; Ortga et al., 2008).

Of the various forms of cyberbullying, the most common cause was social exclusion in an online environment (I ignored some of my classmates in an online environment.) (primary school: 33.2%, secondary school: 40.6%).

This was followed by harassment using a mobile phone (primary school: 22.5%, secondary school: 25.2%).

Among primary school students, hacking an online account (10.4%) and among secondary school students, sending offensive pictures and messages (10.4%) were also often reported.

The higher prevalence of each form of bullying in secondary schools corroborates the findings of Williams and Guerra (2007) who also showed a higher prevalence of cyberbullying in secondary schools.

Examining the prevalence of each type of harassment by gender, we can observe the very same trend across the sample for both genders.

Both girls and boys were most likely to experience social exclusion in an online environment and harassment using a mobile phone.

There has been no significant difference in the proportions compared to the whole sample.

The least common forms of cyberbullying were creating a website or a blog assuming the identity of another person to discredit the victim (primary school: 1.6%, secondary school: 0.8%) and misinform the ISP to exclude the victim (primary school: 2.5%, secondary school: 1.3%).

Examining the least commonly used harassment forms, we have found the very same trend across the sample for both genders.

In their research, Dehue et al. (2008) found that boys are more likely to use different types of cyberbullying than girls.

Our research corroborates this. Among primary school boys, we have found that 12 out of the 14 types of cyberbullying were significantly more common than among girls. The exceptions were the two most common forms of cyberbullying, social exclusion in an online environment and harassment using a mobile phone, with members of both genders being equally prone to.

Secondary school boys were significantly more likely than secondary school girls to send hostile and harassing electronic messages, to edit and share offensive pictures, videos, to distribute secrets or confidential information, to hack online accounts, blogs, or disable access to them.

Examined by school type, we have found out that while primary school boys were prone to spreading malicious rumours, secondary school students were significantly more likely to exercise online social exclusion.

The results of our research show that a high percentage of adolescent young people become victims of cyberbullying. 68.9% of primary school students and 72.4% of secondary school students have already been victims of cyberbullying.

This prevalence value is also slightly higher than previous research in this age group (Patchin and Hinduja, 2006; Ybarra et al., 2007; Raskauskas and Stoltz, 2007; Arıcak 2009).

Examining the process of becoming a victim of cyberbullying, we have found out that the most common form of cyberbullying was harassment using a mobile phone (28%

primary school, 27.3% secondary school).

This was followed by the experience of social exclusion in an online environment (primary school: 23.5%, secondary school: 20.3%) and receiving offensive emails (primary: 13.4%, secondary school: 10%).

Among primary school students, unauthorized sharing of personal information about the victim (11.8%), and among secondary school students, sharing offensive images and messages (10%) were also more common.

If we examine the prevalence of suffering each type of harassment by gender, we can observe the very same trend across the sample for both genders.

Both girls and boys were most likely to be bullied on mobile phones, to be socially excluded from the online environment, and to receive abusive e-mails. There was no significant difference in the proportions compared to the whole sample.

Students have become victims of the following types of cyberbullying least frequently: creating a discrediting website or blog (primary school: 2.3%, secondary school: 0.8%), false complaint exclusion from an online service (primary school:

2.6%, secondary school: 2.1%), and hacking and modifying a personal website or blog (primary school: 3.6%, secondary school: 2.9%).

In terms of gender, we have also found out the very same trend across the sample regarding the least commonly experienced forms of cyberbullying.

According to the results of our research, primary school boys have been significantly more often victimized by the following forms of cyberbullying than girls: hacking an online account or a blog, disabling access, creating a fake website or blog, online impersonation, falsely informing an ISP.

Among secondary school students, we have found no significant difference between the two genders in terms of experiencing specific forms of cyberbullying.

Examined by school type, we have found no significant difference between primary and secondary school students in terms of exposure to each form of cyberbullying.

In summary, our research findings point to the increasing presence of cyberbullying in primary and secondary schools and point to the need to pay much more attention to this phenomenon in schools in the future.

References

Adams, C. (2010): Cyberbullying: How to Make It Stop. 120(2): 44-49.

Arıcak, O. T. (2009). Psychiatric symptomatology as a predictor of cyberbullying among university students. Eurasian Journal of Educational Research, 34, 167–184.

Aricak, T., Siyahaan, S., Uzunhasanoglu, A., Saribeyoglu, S., Ciplak, S., Yilmaz, N., et al. (2008). Cyberbullying among Turkish adolescents. CyberPsychology & Behavior, 11, 253–261.

Belsey, B. (2007). Cyberbullying: a real and growing threat. ATA Magazine, 88(1), 14–21.

Björkqvist, K. (2001). Different names, same issue. Social Development, 10, 272–274.

Crick, N. R. (1995). Relational aggression: The role of intent attributions, feelings of distress, and provocation type. Development and Psychopathology, 7, 313–322.

Dehue, F., Bolman, C., Völlink, T. (2008). Cyberbullying: Youngsters' experiences and parental perception. CyberPsychology & Behavior, 11, 217–223.

Dilmaç, B. (2009). Psychological needs as a predictor of cyber bullying: a preliminary report on college students. Educational Sciences: Theory & Practice, 9 (3), 1307–1325.

Erdur-Baker, Ö, és Kavsut, F. (2007). Cyberbullying. A new face of peer bullying. Eurasian Journal of Educational Research, 27, 31–42.

Galen, B. R., és Underwood, M. K. (1997). A developmental investigation of social aggression among children. Developmental Psychology, 33, 589–600.

Harman, J. P., Hansen, C. E., Conchran, M. E., Lindsey, C. Liar, l. (2005).: Internet faking but not frequency of use affects social skills, self esteem, social anxiety, and aggression. CyberPsychology & Behavior, 8, 1.

Hanewald, R. (2008): Confronting the pedagogical challenge of cyber safety. Australian Journal for Teacher Education 33(3), 1-16.

Hinduja S., és Patchin, J.W. (2008). Cyberbullying: An exploratory analysis of factors related to offending and victimization. Deviant Behavior, 29, 129–156.

Humphrey, N. és Symes, W. (2010) Perceptions of social support and experience of bullying among pupils with Autistic Spectrum Disorders in mainstream secondary schools. European Journal of Special Needs Education 25(1): 77-91.

Keith, S., és Martin, M. E. (2005). Cyber bullying: creating culture of respect in a cyber world. Reclaiming Children and Youth, 13(4), 224–228.

Kowalski, R. M., és Limber, P. (2007). Electronic bullying among middle school students. Journal of Adolscent Healt, 41, 522–530.

Kowalski, R. M., Limber, P., Agatston, P. W. (2008). Cyberbullying: Bullying in the digital age. Molden, MA: Blackwell Publishing.

Lacey, B. (2007). Social aggression: a study of internet harassment. Doctoral Dissertation, Long Island University.

Langos, C. és Sarre, R. (2015): Responding to cyberbullying: The case for family conferencing. Deaking Law Review 20/299.

Li, Q. (2005). Cyber harassment: a study of new method for an old behavior. Journal of Educational Computing Research, 32(3), 265–277

Li, Q. (2006). Cyberbullying in schools. A research of gender differences. School Psychology International, 27, 157–170.

Li, Q. (2007). New bottle but old wine: A research of cyberbullying in schools. Computers in Human Behavior, 23, 1777–1791.

Ortega, R., Mora-Merchán, J. A., Jäger, T. (Eds.). (2007). Acting against school bullying and violence. The role of media, local authorities and the Internet [E-Book]. Landau: Verlag Empirische Pädagogik.

Ortega, R., Calmaestra, J., Mora-Merchán, J. (2008). Cyberbullying: un estudio exploratorio en educación secundaria. International Journal of Psychology and Psychological Therapy, 8, 183–192.

Ponsford, J. (2007). The future of adolescent female cyber-bullying: electronic media's effect on aggressive female communication. Texas State Universty, Texas.

Riebel J., Jager R.S., Fischer U.C. (2009): Cyberbullying in Germany – an exploration of prevalence, overlapping with real life bullying and coping strategies. Psychology Science Quarterly, Volume 51, 2009 (3), pp. 298-314.

Shariff, S., Gouin, R. (2005). Cyber-dilemmas: Gendered hierarchies free expression and cyber-safety in schools. Paper presented at safety and security in a networked world: Balancing cyber-rights and responsibilities. Oxford Internet Institute Conference, on September 8, Oxford, U.K.

Slonje, R., és Smith, P. K. (2008). Cyberbullying: another main type of bullying? Scandinavian Journal of Psychology, 49, 147–154.

Slonje, R., Smith, P. K. Frisén, A. (2013) The nature of cyberbullying and strategies for prevention. Computers in Human Behavior 29 (1): 26-32.

Smith, P. K., Mahdavi, J., Carvalho, M., Fisher, S., Russell, S., Tippett, N. (2008). Cyberbullying: Its nature and impact in secondary school pupils. Journal of Child Psychology and Psychiatry, 49(4), 376-385.

Ybarra, M. L., és Mitchell, K. J. (2004). Online aggressors/targets, aggressors, and targets: A comparison of associated youth characteristics. Journal of Child Psychology and Psychiatry, 45, 1308–1316.

Ybarra, M. L., Espelage, D. L., Mitchell, K. J. (2007). The co-occurrence of Internet harassment and unwanted sexual solicitation victimization and perpetration: associations with psychosocial indictors. Journal of Adolescent Health, 41(6), 31–41.

Ybarra, M., West, M. D., Leaf, P. (2007). Examining the overlap in Internet harassment and school bullying: implications for school intervention. Journal of Adolescent Health, 41, 42–50.

Vandebosch, H. és Cleemput, K. V. (2008): Definig Cyberbulying: A Qualitative Research into the Perceptions of Youngsters. 11(4): 499-503.

Willard, N. E. (2006). Cyberbullying and Cyberthreats: Responding to the challenge of online social cruelty, threats, and distress. Eugene, Oregon: Center for Safe and Responsible Internet Use.

Williams, K. R., és Guerra, N. G. (2007). Prevalence and predictors of internet bullying. Journal of Adolescent Health, 41, 14–21.

Appendix

Cyber Bully Scale

In this questionnaire, you will find statements that refer to behaviours that you experience when you are using your phone and the Internet. There are four options for each statement:

almost never (0), sometimes (1), often (2), almost always (3)

Please read each statement carefully and then tick the number of the question that you believe best suits your behaviour in such situations.

1	I sent emails to some of my classmates in which I mocked or made them uncomfortable.	0	1	2	3
2	I uploaded videos about some of my classmates to You Tube that were funny for the others.	0	1	2	3
3	When I became aware of them, I was happy to share the secrets of others on the net.	0	1	2	3
4	I sent an annoying anonymous message to one of my classmates (text, picture, video) via email, SMS, chat or social network site.	0	1	2	3

5	I logged into the personal user account of one of my classmates (email, social network, etc.)	0	1	2	3
6	I impersonated the online personality of one of my classmates (email, community site, etc.).	0	1	2	3
7	I edited a picture or video of one of my classmates that puts him or her in a ridiculous, humiliating position, and distributed it online.	0	1	2	3
8	I have already called my classmate anonymously on a mobile phone.	0	1	2	3
9	I created a website or blog about one of my classmates in order to discredit him or her to others.	0	1	2	3
10	I hacked and modified a personal website or blog of one of my classmates.	0	1	2	3
11	I falsely informed an ISP to exclude one of my classmates from the online service.	0	1	2	3
12	I spread malicious rumors about my classmates using online tools.	0	1	2	3

13	I blocked one of my classmate's online access- for example, by changing the password.	0	1	2	3
14	I ignored some of my classmates in an online environment.	0	1	2	3

„*Before finishing, please make sure you have answered all statements.*"

Cyber Victim Scale

In this questionnaire, you will find statements that refer to behaviours that you experience when you are using your phone and the Internet. There are four options for each statement:

almost never (0), sometimes (1), often (2), almost always (3)

Please read each statement carefully and then tick the number of the question that you believe best suits your behaviour in such situations.

1	I received emails from some of my classmates that offended me.	0	1	2	3
2	My classmates have already uploaded a video of me to YouTube that made me feel uncomfortable.	0	1	2	3
3	Some information about me has been uploaded to the net that I would not have liked if others knew about it.	0	1	2	3
4	I received an anonymous message containing harassing content from one of my classmates (text, picture, video) via email, SMS, chat or community site.	0	1	2	3

5	One of my classmates has logged in to my personal user account (email, social network, etc.).	0	1	2	3
6	One of my classmates faked my online personality (email, social network, etc.).	0	1	2	3
7	One of my classmates has already edited a picture or video of me that put me in a ridiculous, humiliating position, and disseminated it online.	0	1	2	3
8	I have already been called anonymously on a mobile phone, about which I thought my classmates were having fun with me.	0	1	2	3
9	One of my classmates has created a website or blog to discredit me to other people.	0	1	2	3
10	My classmates hacked my personal website or blog and modified it.	0	1	2	3
11	I have been excluded from an online service because I was falsely reported to the service provider.	0	1	2	3
12	My classmates have been spreading malicious rumours about me using online tools.	0	1	2	3

13	My classmate blocked my online access - for example, by changing the password.	0	1	2	3
14	Some of my classmates ignored me in an online enviromnment.	0	1	2	3

„Before finishing, please make sure you have answered all statements."